THE HOLISTIC COW

A LOOK AT THE PHYSICAL, SPIRITUAL, AND CULTURAL IMPORTANCE OF COWS IN INDIA

DR. JAGADEESH PILLAI

|| Dedicated to All "Divine Mothe Cow" Lovers Around The World ||

Contents

Contents

Prayer

Sarvakaamdudhe devi sarvatithirbhishechini |

Pavane surbhi shreshte devi tubhyam namostute |

About The Author

Dr. Jagadeesh Pillai is a renowned Guinness World Record holder, writer, and researcher hailing from Varanasi, also known as the abode of Lord Shiva. With a Ph.D. in Vedic Science and a range of creative ideas and achievements, he is a true polymath. Although his roots can be traced back to Kerala, the people of Varanasi hold him in high regard and affectionately consider him one of their own.

Dr. Pillai has achieved four Guinness World Records in the following subjects:

1. "Script to Screen" - In this record, Dr. Pillai produced and directed an animation film within the shortest time possible, breaking the previous record set by Canadians. He has also received numerous national and international awards and recognitions for this achievement.

2. Longest Line of Postcards - For this record, Dr. Pillai created a line of 16,300 postcards on the occasion of the 163rd anniversary of Indian Postal Day. The event also included a questionnaire about the Indian flag.

3. Largest Poster Awareness Campaign - Dr. Pillai designed an awareness campaign on the subject of "Beti Bachao - Beti Padhao" (Save the Girl Child - Educate the Girl Child) to achieve this record.

4. Largest Envelope - In tribute to the Indian Prime Minister's "Make in India" initiative, Dr. Pillai created a 4000 square meter envelope using waste paper to achieve this record.

5. Attempted - 70000 Candles on a 210 kg Cake - To celebrate the 70th Indian Independence Day, Dr. Pillai attempted to light 70,000 candles on a 210 kg cake, which was recorded in World Records India.

6. Attempted - Documentary on Dhamek Stupa of Sarnath in 17 Languages - Dr. Pillai attempted to create a documentary on the Dhamek Stupa of Sarnath, dubbing it in 17 different languages. The result of this attempt is currently awaiting confirmation from the Guinness World Records.

He is versatile in Gita teaching. The young generation is fond of his Gita teaching and he has changed the life of many young through his continued motivational boost up and teachings.

He has composed and sung Gayatri Mantra in 1008 different tunes.

He has composed and sung Hanuman Chalisa in 108 different tunes.

He has composed and sung hundreds of Sanskrit Bhajans, Patriotic songs, etc.

He has written and directed so many short films and documentaries for awareness campaigns.

He has done voluntary services to UP Police and Kerala Police to spread awareness campaigns on the various issue through videos and photography.

He is on the path of authoring thousands of books on Indian culture, Indian Temples, and the life of extraordinary people.

It is hard to believe that he has produced and directed more than 100 Documentaries on a particular city (Varanasi) which is done by a single person.

He has helped and guided more than 25 boys and girls to achieve world records through various creative and innovative methods.

A multifaceted person who can apply the best of his intellect using the God-given blessings which have been showered upon every human being granting them an immense capacity to learn, experience, and experiment with many things and do wonders in this world of discrimination and disparities.

He is a teacher and a student at the same time who always learns every day and teaches every day. As a master, his weakness was that he never sticks to a particular subject.

Perhaps this weakness gives him the strength to master any area which he came across.

Each of his days dawned with learning a new topic and he spend most of his time experimenting and researching it.

He is also a selfless social activist and a motivational speaker.

His life was full of struggle, ups and downs, and failures. But he never gave up and faced all his trials and tribulations full of confidence. Today he is a successful young man with a lot of enthusiasm and rich life experience.

He is an efficient Tarot Card Reader, Astro-Vastu Consultant and an excellent singer and composer.

He has sung full Ram Charita Manas 138 hours audio by his own composition. He has also sung the whole Bhagavad-Gita in his own composition with a rhythmic background.

He has also sung "Lokah Samastha Sukhino Bhavantu" in 50 different languages.

Currently working on a detailed and scientific study on Veda, Upanishad, Puranas, Bhagavad Gita, etc.

He has composed and sung Hanuman Chalisa in 108 different compositions and Gayatri Mantra in 1008 different compositions.

<u>Awards</u>

Four Times Guinness World Records, Winner of Mahatma Gandhi Vishwa Shanti Puraskar , Mahatma Gandhi Global Peace Ambassador, Kashi Ratna Award, Dr. APJ Abdul Kalam Motivational Person of the Year 2017, Mother Teresa Award, Indira Gandhi Priyadarshini Award, Bharat Vikas Ratna Award, Udyog Ratna Award, Vigyan Prasar Award, Poorvanchal Ratn Samman.

Preface

The cow is a sacred and revered animal in many Indian belief systems, including Hinduism, Jainism, and Sikhism. In these belief systems, cows are seen as a symbol of wealth, prosperity, and non-violence, and are revered for their ability to nourish and sustain life.

Cows play a central role in the daily lives of many people in India, where they are used as a source of labor for plowing fields and as a source of transportation. Cows are also an important source of milk, butter, and cheese, which are a staple in the Indian diet. Cow dung is also used as a natural fertilizer for crops and as a natural fuel for cooking and lighting fires.

In Hinduism, cows are closely connected to the goddess Lakshmi, the deity of wealth, prosperity, and good fortune, and are associated with the concept of the "cow of plenty," a celestial cow that is believed to be able to give anything a person desires. Cows are also seen as a symbol of the cycle of life and are closely connected to the concept of reincarnation.

In times of turmoil and unrest, faith provides a comforting source of support and connection to something greater. It's a light of hope even amidst the darkness.

However, with so many faith-based belief systems in practice throughout the world, it can be difficult to understand their origins and how they can be embraced in one's own lives.

This book bridges such a divide by providing an overview of the Hindu Cow based belief system. Often referred to as Gaushala Dharma, this revered sect of faith is over five thousand years old, and much beloved to many worldwide. It has its roots in ancient Indian texts and has been the foundation of sacred love for animals, primarily the cow, throughout civilization.

From its history to its spiritual principles, this book covers a broad range of topics, such as the five major aspects of Gaushal Dharma and the various ritualistic practices that have evolved over time. It also delves into the ethical, economic, and environmental benefits to society that stem from the adherence to this belief system. Lastly, the book explores the critical role of cows in the Hindu faith, including the influential elements they play within the Temple Festivals and their protective symbolism.

Although this book explains the beliefs in the Gaushala Dharma faith, it is not intended to take the place of actual practice. Instead, it serves as an introduction and a resource for further exploration by the reader's own faith. It is hoped that by delving into the history and understanding the meaning behind this belief system many spiritual seekers will find the guidance, actionable insights, as well as the ultimate connection to something sacred and of greater significance.

This book endeavors to enlighten and inspire its readers with the ancient and deeply profound faith of Gaushala Dharma. May the reader gain a greater understanding of this unique belief system and use the acquired knowledge for their life's path.

CHAPTER ONE

Kamadhenu

Kamadhenu, also known as the ancestor of all cows, is considered a divine and wish-fulfilling animal in Hinduism. The Vedas, ancient Hindu scriptures, describe Kamadhenu as a cow that contains all the gods, goddesses, and the Trinity within her and brings good fortune to those who worship her. In Hindu tradition, worshipping Kamadhenu or cows in general is believed to purify one of their sins, both current and past. Kamadhenu is mentioned in various Vedic scriptures, including the Bhagwad Gita and the Mahabharata, and is revered as Homadhenu, a source of commodities like clarified butter and milk used in Vedic fire sacrifices. While it is rare to find a temple dedicated solely to Kamadhenu, cows are often revered as her physical embodiment and are held in high esteem by Hindus.

Per folklore, it is said that Kamadhenu once visited the ashram of sage Vasishta and granted a child to King Dilipan, who had been childless, after the king followed the sage's advice to worship Kamadhenu. This story is believed to be the basis for the rituals and puja (worship) practices involving cows that are still performed today. The Skanda Purana, a Hindu scripture, contains a chapter called

"Grihasta Ashrama" which provides a summary of the positions of various deities, sages, and Vedas within the body of a cow. In this chapter, Maharishi Veda Vyas extols the virtues of human beings, especially Brahmanas, who are considered to play a key role in performing duties towards gods, ancestors, fellow humans, and various other beings including insects, birds, and even demons.

In Hinduism, cows are often seen as symbols of virtues and are traditionally cared for by Brahmanas, a class of priests or intellectuals. According to Hindu mythology, the Rig Veda is represented by the back of cows, the Yajur Veda by their middle portion, and the Sama Veda by their stomach. The horns of cows are seen as representing ishta (sacrifices) and apurti (abundance), while the body hairs are seen as representing the Veda Suktas (hymns). The dung and urine of cows are associated with shanti karma (peaceful actions) and pushti karma (nourishing actions), and their feet are seen as representing the Aksharas (letters of the Sanskrit alphabet). Cows are also believed to live for the sake of the various mantras (sacred sounds or phrases) associated with their pada-krama-jata-and ghana paatha (ritualistic steps). According to Hindu belief, cows have four nipples on their breasts, each representing different deities and beings: Devatas, Pitras, Bhutas, Rishis, Munis, and Sureswaraganas. The last nipple is believed to yield the most milk for human consumption. Thus, it is considered the responsibility of human beings to take care of cows.

In Hinduism, cows are considered sacred animals and are often given special treatment in the form of puja (worship).

There are certain days of the week that are associated with

specific benefits that can be obtained through cow puja.

For example, on

Monday, giving grass, food, agathi keerai (a type of leafy vegetable), and banana to a cow is believed to help purify one of mathru (mother) and pithru (father) dosha (negative energies).

On Tuesday, giving food and water to a cow is thought to bring opportunities for purchasing housing and land.

On Wednesday, giving food to a cow is believed to bring advancement in one's professional life.

On Thursday, offering rice porridge to a cow is said to remove the negative effects of purva jenma (past life) dosha.

On Friday, doing cow puja is believed to bring the blessings of Sri Mahalakshmi, a Hindu goddess of wealth and prosperity.

On Saturday, giving grass and agathi keerai to a cow is said to remove one from the grips of poverty. On Thuvathisi (a day of the week in the Tamil calendar), worshipping a cow and offering food is believed to provide the punya (merit) of annathanam (feeding the hungry) to 1000 people.

CHAPTER TWO

Gopashtami

Gopashtami is a Hindu festival that celebrates cows and is observed annually across India. It falls in the month of Karthika and is dedicated to Lord Krishna, who is known as Gopala or the caretaker of cows.

According to Hindu mythology, Lord Krishna lifted the hill Govardhana to protect the cows and the people of Vrindavan from the wrath of Indra, the king of gods. Krishna held the mountain with his little finger for seven days straight, from the first day of the Kartik shukla paksha (bright lunar fortnight) to the seventh day, known as saptami. On the eighth day, Indra realized his mistake and apologized to Krishna.

On Gopashtami, cows are decorated and offered jaggery, rice, water, and grass as a way of expressing gratitude to them. Cow milk is considered the closest alternative to human milk for human newborns, and cow products such as cow urine and cow dung are used in Ayurveda, an ancient Hindu system of medicine. In Hindu tradition, it is believed that applying the soil from underneath a cow's feet on the forehead (called Guadhuli) can help remove financial problems.

Gopashtami is predominantly celebrated in the northern part of India, while in the south, the festival of Thai Pongal is celebrated with similar rituals. Thai Pongal is a harvest festival that is oriented towards worshipping the sun god and the land that provides for all living beings. The second day of Thai Pongal, known as Maatu Pongal, is dedicated to cows, who are decorated and offered the best food as a way of thanking them for their contributions to farmers.

In ancient times, cows and bulls played a crucial role in agriculture, and the festival of Jallikattu or Manji Virattu was held to honor them. However, the current form of the festival has been criticized for being violent and causing harm to cows and humans.

Cows are considered important from an economic standpoint in Hinduism, as they provide numerous products that are beneficial to people of all ages. Hindus are taught to be gentle and caring towards cows, as they are seen as surrogate mothers. The products of cows, including milk, ghee, and yogurt, are believed to have medicinal properties and are used in various rituals and ceremonies.

CHAPTER THREE

The Holistic Cow

"The Holistic Cow: A Look at the Physical, Spiritual, and Cultural Importance of Cows in India"

In Hinduism, the cow is considered a symbol of wealth, strength, and motherly love. Cows are also associated with the Hindu god Krishna, who is often depicted playing the flute to a group of cows and cowherders. In Hindu mythology, cows are believed to be able to give anything to a person, including knowledge, wealth, and strength. This is why the cow is often referred to as "Gau Mata," or "Mother Cow."

One of the main reasons the cow is held in such high regard in Hinduism is due to its associations with the divine. In Hindu mythology, the cow is seen as a symbol of the earth, and is referred to as "Aditi," the mother of all the gods. The cow is also associated with the Hindu goddess Lakshmi, the deity of wealth, prosperity, and good fortune.

In Hinduism, the cow is also seen as a symbol of non-violence and selfless giving. The cow is revered for its ability to nourish and sustain life, as it provides milk, butter, cheese, and yogurt, as well as serving as a means of transportation and a source of plowing fields. In Hindu tradition, cows are not to be harmed or killed for food or any other reason, and harming a cow is considered a sin.

In addition to its spiritual and cultural significance, the cow is also seen as a symbol of prosperity in Hinduism. In Hindu mythology, the cow is seen as a symbol of the earth's bounty and is believed to bring good fortune to those who possess and care for it. The cow is also seen as a symbol of abundance and fertility, and is often depicted with the Hindu god Kamadeva, the deity of love and desire.

In Hindu tradition, the cow is also seen as a symbol of Motherly love and is often depicted with the Hindu goddess Annapurna, the deity of nourishment. Cows are believed to be able to give anything to a person, including knowledge, wealth, and strength, and are therefore seen as a symbol of selfless giving and nurturing.

Overall, the cow holds a central and revered place in Hinduism, and is seen as a symbol of wealth, strength, non-violence, selfless giving, and motherly love.

CHAPTER FOUR

The Role of Cows in Vedic rituals

In Vedic tradition, cows played a central role in many rituals and ceremonies. Cows were often seen as a symbol of wealth and were given as gifts to the gods during ceremonies as a sign of devotion. Cows were also used as offerings in the yajna, a sacred fire ritual, and their milk and ghee (clarified butter) were used in many Vedic rituals as a means of purification.

One of the most important roles of cows in Vedic rituals was their use in the ashvamedha, a royal rite in which a consecrated horse was released to roam freely for a year, accompanied by a retinue of followers. At the end of the year, the horse was brought back and a sacrifice was made to the gods. The ashvamedha was a symbol of the king's sovereignty and was believed to bring prosperity to the kingdom. Cows played a central role in the ashvamedha, as they were often given as offerings to the gods during the sacrifice.

In addition to their use in Vedic rituals, cows were also seen as a source of nourishment and sustenance in Vedic society.

Cows provided milk, butter, and cheese, which were an important part of the Vedic diet, and their dung was used as fuel for cooking and for lighting fires in temples.

Overall, cows played a significant and revered role in Vedic rituals and ceremonies, and were seen as a symbol of wealth, prosperity, and nourishment.

CHAPTER FIVE

The Divine Status of Cows in the Bhagavad Gita

In the Bhagavad Gita, a Hindu scripture, cows are given a divine status and are seen as symbols of prosperity and abundance. In the text, Lord Krishna, an avatar of the Hindu god Vishnu, advises the warrior Arjuna to offer cows as gifts to the gods and to the brahmins, as they are believed to bring blessings and prosperity.

Lord Krishna also speaks of the importance of cow protection in the Bhagavad Gita, stating that those who harm cows and cause them suffering will incur sin. In Hindu tradition, cows are seen as a symbol of non-violence and selfless giving, and harming a cow is considered a grave offense.

In the Bhagavad Gita, Lord Krishna also speaks of the cow's association with the earth and the nourishing qualities of its milk. Cows are seen as a symbol of the earth's bounty and are believed to bring good fortune to those who possess and care for them.

Overall, the Bhagavad Gita highlights the divine status of cows in Hinduism and the importance of protecting and caring for them.

CHAPTER SIX

Cows as Symbols of Prosperity in Hindu Mythology

In Hindu mythology, cows are seen as symbols of prosperity and abundance. Cows are believed to bring good fortune and blessings to those who possess and care for them, and are often depicted with the Hindu goddess Lakshmi, the deity of wealth, prosperity, and good fortune.

In Hindu tradition, cows are also seen as a symbol of the earth's bounty and are associated with the concept of the "cow of plenty," a celestial cow that is believed to be able to give anything a person desires. The cow is also seen as a symbol of fertility and is often depicted with the Hindu god Kamadeva, the deity of love and desire.

In Hindu mythology, cows are also associated with the myth of the "churning of the ocean," in which the gods and demons worked together to churn the oceans in order to obtain the elixir of immortality. During the churning, the cow Surabhi emerged from the oceans, symbolizing the abundance and prosperity that comes from hard work and collaboration.

Overall, cows are seen as symbols of prosperity and abundance in Hindu mythology, and are associated with the concepts of wealth, fertility, and the earth's bounty.

CHAPTER SEVEN

The Cow as a Symbol of Selfless Giving in Hinduism

In Hinduism, the cow is seen as a symbol of selfless giving and nurturing. Cows are believed to be able to give anything to a person, including knowledge, wealth, and strength, and are therefore referred to as "Gau Mata," or "Mother Cow."

Cows are also seen as a symbol of non-violence and selflessness, as they are not to be harmed or killed for food or any other reason. In Hindu tradition, harming a cow is considered a sin, as cows are revered for their ability to nourish and sustain life.

In Hindu mythology, the cow is also associated with the goddess Annapurna, the deity of nourishment. Cows are believed to be able to provide nourishment in the form of milk, butter, cheese, and yogurt, and are therefore seen as a symbol of maternal love and care.

Overall, the cow is seen as a symbol of selfless giving and

nurturing in Hinduism, and is revered for its ability to nourish and sustain life.

CHAPTER EIGHT

Cows in Jainism: Ahimsa and Non-Violence

In Jainism, cows are revered for their principles of non-violence and non-injury (ahimsa). Jains believe that all living beings, including cows, have an eternal soul and should be treated with respect and compassion. As such, Jains adhere to a strict vegetarian diet and abstain from consuming meat, including beef.

Jains also follow the principle of non-possession, and believe that it is wrong to own or exploit living beings for personal gain. In Jain tradition, cows are not to be used for labor or milk production, and Jains who own cows do so for the purpose of protecting and caring for them.

Cows are also seen as a symbol of non-violence and ahimsa in Jainism. In Jain mythology, the first Jain tirthankara, or spiritual teacher, was born as a cow in one of his past lives. This emphasis on the cow as a symbol of non-violence and compassion is reflected in the Jain practice of offering food and care to cows as a way of accumulating merit and purifying the soul.

Overall, cows hold a significant place in Jainism, and are revered for their principles of non-violence and non-injury.

CHAPTER NINE

The Role of Cows in Sikhism

In Sikhism, cows are seen as a symbol of selfless giving and are revered for their ability to nourish and sustain life. Sikhs believe that all living beings have an equal right to live and should be treated with compassion and respect. As such, Sikhs follow a vegetarian diet and abstain from consuming meat, including beef.

Cows are also seen as a symbol of the Gurus' selfless service in Sikhism. The Gurus, or spiritual teachers, of Sikhism believed in the importance of selfless service and often used the metaphor of the cow to illustrate this concept. In Sikh mythology, the Gurus are said to have cared for and protected cows just as they cared for and protected their own children.

In Sikh tradition, cows are also seen as a symbol of prosperity and abundance. The Guru Granth Sahib, the holy scripture of Sikhism, states that those who care for cows will prosper, and that the milk of the cow is a blessing from God.

Overall, cows hold a significant place in Sikhism and are seen as a symbol of selfless giving, nourishment, and prosperity.

CHAPTER TEN

The Significance of Cow Dung in Hinduism

In Hinduism, cow dung is seen as a sacred and purifying substance. Cow dung is believed to have antimicrobial properties and is used in Hindu rituals and practices as a means of purification and protection.

One of the main uses of cow dung in Hinduism is as a natural disinfectant. Cow dung is often used to clean and purify floors, walls, and other surfaces in Hindu homes and temples, as it is believed to have the ability to kill germs and bacteria. Cow dung is also used as a natural insect repellent and is believed to keep away insects and other pests.

In Hindu ritual practices, cow dung is also used as an offering to the gods. In the puja, a Hindu worship ritual, cow dung is often used as a symbol of the earth and is placed on the altar as an offering to the gods. Cow dung is also used in the yajna, a sacred fire ritual, as a fuel for the sacred fire.

Cow dung is also used in Hindu tradition for medicinal purposes. Cow dung is believed to have healing properties and is used in Ayurvedic medicine as a treatment for various ailments, including skin conditions and respiratory problems.

Overall, cow dung holds a significant place in Hinduism and is seen as a sacred and purifying substance with a variety of uses.

CHAPTER ELEVEN

The Role of Cow Urine in Ayurvedic Medicine

In Ayurvedic medicine, cow urine is believed to have medicinal properties and is used as a treatment for a variety of ailments. Cow urine is believed to have detoxifying and purifying properties and is used as a natural disinfectant.

Cow urine is also used in Ayurvedic medicine as a treatment for various skin conditions, including acne and eczema. It is believed to have anti-inflammatory and antimicrobial properties and is applied topically to the skin to treat these conditions.

In addition to its use as a skin treatment, cow urine is also used in Ayurvedic medicine to treat respiratory conditions such as asthma and bronchitis. It is believed to have expectorant properties and is used to loosen phlegm and clear the respiratory tract.

Cow urine is also used in Ayurvedic medicine as a general tonic to improve overall health and well-being. It is believed to boost the immune system and to have a positive effect on the digestive system.

Overall, cow urine plays a significant role in Ayurvedic medicine and is believed to have a variety of medicinal properties.

CHAPTER TWELVE

"The Symbolic Meaning of the Colors of Cows in Hinduism"

"The Symbolic Meaning of the Colors of Cows in Hinduism"In Hinduism, the color of a cow can hold symbolic meaning. White cows are often seen as a symbol of purity and are associated with the Hindu goddess Lakshmi, the deity of wealth, prosperity, and good fortune. White cows are also seen as a symbol of the moon and are believed to bring calmness and peace.

Black cows are often seen as a symbol of strength and are associated with the Hindu god Shiva, the deity of destruction and regeneration. Black cows are also seen as a symbol of the earth and are believed to be able to give anything a person desires.

Red cows are often seen as a symbol of passion and are associated with the Hindu god Kamadeva, the deity of love and desire. Red cows are also seen as a symbol of fertility and are believed to bring abundance and prosperity.

Yellow cows are often seen as a symbol of knowledge and are associated with the Hindu goddess Saraswati, the deity of knowledge and wisdom. Yellow cows are also seen as a symbol of the sun and are believed to bring energy and vitality.

Overall, the color of a cow can hold symbolic meaning in Hinduism, and is often associated with specific deities and qualities.

CHAPTER THIRTEEN

The Mythical Birth of the Cow Surabhi in Hinduism

In Hindu mythology, the cow Surabhi is a celestial cow who is believed to have emerged from the oceans during the "churning of the ocean" myth. According to the myth, the gods and demons worked together to churn the oceans in order to obtain the elixir of immortality. During the churning, a number of celestial objects and beings emerged from the oceans, including the cow Surabhi.

Surabhi is considered to be the mother of all cows and is revered for her ability to give anything a person desires. She is often depicted with the Hindu god Krishna, who is said to have taken care of her and protected her from harm.

In Hindu tradition, the cow Surabhi is seen as a symbol of abundance and prosperity, and is believed to bring blessings and good fortune to those who possess and care for her. Surabhi is also seen as a symbol of the earth's bounty and is associated with the concept of the "cow of plenty," a celestial cow that is believed to be able to give anything a person desires.

Overall, the cow Surabhi holds a significant place in Hindu mythology and is revered as a symbol of abundance and prosperity.

CHAPTER FOURTEEN

The Worship of Cows in Tribal Belief Systems in India

In many tribal belief systems in India, cows are held in high regard and are often the focus of worship and veneration. In these belief systems, cows are seen as a symbol of wealth and prosperity and are believed to bring blessings and good fortune to those who possess and care for them.

In some tribal belief systems, cows are also seen as a symbol of the earth and are associated with the concept of the "mother cow," a deity who is believed to be able to give anything a person desires. Cows are often depicted with this deity and are believed to be able to provide nourishment and sustenance.

In addition to their use in worship, cows also play a central role in the daily lives of many tribal communities in India. Cows are often used as a source of milk, butter, and cheese, and their dung is used as fuel for cooking and for lighting fires in homes and temples.

Overall, cows hold a significant place in many tribal belief systems in India and are revered as a symbol of wealth, prosperity, and the earth's bounty.

CHAPTER FIFTEEN

The Role of Cows in Indian Agriculture and Sustainability

Cows play a significant role in Indian agriculture and sustainability. In rural areas of India, cows are often used as a source of labor for plowing fields and as a source of transportation. Cows are also used to produce milk, butter, and cheese, which are an important part of the Indian diet.

In addition to their use in agriculture, cows also play a role in sustainability in India. Cow dung is used as a natural fertilizer for crops and is an important source of organic matter for the soil. Cow dung is also used as a natural fuel for cooking and for lighting fires, which helps to reduce the reliance on non-renewable energy sources.

Cows play a significant role in Indian agriculture and sustainability, and are an important part of rural life in India.

CHAPTER SIXTEEN

The Cow as a Symbol of Motherly Love in Hinduism

In Hinduism, the cow is seen as a symbol of motherly love and care. Cows are often referred to as "Gau Mata," or "Mother Cow," and are believed to be able to give anything to a person, including knowledge, wealth, and strength.

In Hindu tradition, cows are also associated with the goddess Annapurna, the deity of nourishment. Cows are believed to be able to provide nourishment in the form of milk, butter, cheese, and yogurt, and are therefore seen as a symbol of maternal love and care.

In Hindu mythology, the cow is also associated with the myth of the "churning of the ocean," in which the gods and demons worked together to churn the oceans in order to obtain the elixir of immortality. During the churning, the cow Surabhi emerged from the oceans, symbolizing the abundance and prosperity that comes from hard work and collaboration.

Overall, the cow is seen as a symbol of motherly love and care in Hinduism, and is revered for its ability to nourish and sustain life.

CHAPTER SEVENTEEN

The Cultural and Social Importance of Cows in India

Cows hold a significant place in Indian culture and society. In Hinduism, cows are seen as a symbol of wealth, prosperity, and non-violence, and are revered for their ability to nourish and sustain life. Cows are also seen as a symbol of the earth's bounty and are associated with the concept of the "cow of plenty," a celestial cow that is believed to be able to give anything a person desires.

In addition to their spiritual and cultural significance, cows also play a central role in the daily lives of many people in India. Cows are often used as a source of labor for plowing fields and as a source of transportation, and their milk, butter, and cheese are an important part of the Indian diet. Cow dung is also used as a natural fuel for cooking and for lighting fires.

Cows hold a significant place in Indian culture and society and play a central role in the daily lives of many people in

India.

CHAPTER EIGHTEEN

The Role of Cows in Indian Festivals and Celebrations

Cows play a significant role in Indian festivals and celebrations. In Hinduism, cows are seen as a symbol of wealth, prosperity, and non-violence, and are revered for their ability to nourish and sustain life. As such, cows are often the focus of worship and veneration during Hindu festivals and celebrations.

One example of this is the festival of Gopashtami, which is dedicated to the worship of cows. During this festival, cows are decorated with flowers and garlands and are offered special prayers and offerings.

Cows are also often the focus of celebrations during the Hindu festival of Janmashtami, which marks the birthday of Lord Krishna. Lord Krishna is often depicted with cows and is said to have taken care of and protected cows during his lifetime.

In addition to their role in Hindu festivals and celebrations, cows also play a central role in the daily lives of many people in India. Cows are often used as a source of labor for plowing fields and as a source of transportation, and their milk, butter, and cheese are an important part of the Indian diet.

Overall, cows hold a significant place in Indian festivals and celebrations, and play a central role in the daily lives of many people in India.

The Cow as a Symbol of Fertility and Abundance in Indian Belief Systems

In many Indian belief systems, cows are seen as a symbol of fertility and abundance. Cows are believed to be able to give anything a person desires, including knowledge, wealth, and strength, and are therefore associated with the concept of the "cow of plenty," a celestial cow that is believed to be able to give anything a person desires.

In Hinduism, cows are also associated with the goddess Annapurna, the deity of nourishment. Cows are believed to be able to provide nourishment in the form of milk, butter, cheese, and yogurt, and are therefore seen as a symbol of fertility and abundance.

In Hindu mythology, the cow is also associated with the myth of the "churning of the ocean," in which the gods and demons worked together to churn the oceans in order to obtain the elixir of immortality. During the churning, the cow Surabhi emerged from the oceans, symbolizing the abundance and prosperity that comes from hard work and collaboration.

Cows are seen as a symbol of fertility and abundance in many Indian belief systems, and are revered for their ability to nourish and sustain life.

CHAPTER TWENTY

The Connection Between Cows and the Hindu Goddess Lakshmi

In Hinduism, the cow is closely connected to the goddess Lakshmi, the deity of wealth, prosperity, and good fortune. Lakshmi is often depicted with cows and is believed to be able to bring blessings and good fortune to those who possess and care for cows.

In Hindu tradition, cows are seen as a symbol of wealth and prosperity, and are associated with the concept of the "cow of plenty," a celestial cow that is believed to be able to give anything a person desires. Cows are also seen as a symbol of non-violence and are believed to bring peace and calmness.

In Hindu mythology, the cow is also associated with the myth of the "churning of the ocean," in which the gods and demons worked together to churn the oceans in order to obtain the elixir of immortality. During the churning, the cow Surabhi emerged from the oceans, symbolizing the abundance and prosperity that comes from hard work and collaboration.

Cows hold a significant place in Hinduism and are closely connected to the goddess Lakshmi, the deity of wealth, prosperity, and good fortune.

CHAPTER TWENTY-ONE

The Symbolism of Cow Bells in Hinduism

In Hinduism, cow bells are seen as a symbol of the divine and are often used in Hindu rituals and ceremonies. Cow bells are believed to have the ability to ward off evil spirits and to bring good fortune, and are therefore considered to be sacred objects.

In Hindu tradition, cow bells are often used during puja, a Hindu worship ritual, as a means of offering devotion to the gods. Cow bells are also used in Hindu temple ceremonies, where they are rung to mark the beginning and end of the ceremony.

Cow bells are also often worn by cows as a symbol of their sacredness. In Hindu tradition, cows are seen as a symbol of non-violence and are believed to bring peace and calmness. Cow bells are therefore worn by cows as a means of protecting them and as a symbol of their divine status.

Cow bells hold a significant place in Hinduism and are seen as a symbol of the divine and a means of protection.

CHAPTER TWENTY-TWO

The Role of Cows in the Hindu Concept of Reincarnation

In Hinduism, cows are seen as a symbol of non-violence and are believed to bring peace and calmness. Cows are also believed to be able to give anything a person desires, including knowledge, wealth, and strength, and are therefore associated with the concept of the "cow of plenty," a celestial cow that is believed to be able to give anything a person desires.

In Hindu tradition, cows are also seen as a symbol of the cycle of life and are closely connected to the concept of reincarnation. According to Hindu belief, the soul is eternal and goes through a cycle of birth, death, and rebirth. Cows are often depicted in Hindu art and literature as a symbol of the cycle of life and are associated with the concept of reincarnation.

In Hindu mythology, the cow is also associated with the myth of the "churning of the ocean," in which the gods and demons worked together to churn the oceans in order to obtain the elixir of immortality. During the churning, the cow Surabhi emerged from the oceans, symbolizing the abundance and prosperity that comes from hard work and collaboration.

Cows hold a significant place in Hinduism and are seen as a symbol of non-violence, abundance, and the cycle of life.

Other Books Of The Author

1. The Moments When I Met God
2. Kashiyile Theertha Pathangal
3. GURU GYAN VANI
4. Abhiprerak Gita
5. ASSI SE JAIN GHAT TAK
6. Hopelessness of Arjuna
7. The Soul and It's True Nature
8. Sense of Action (Karma)
9. Action through Wisdom
10. Action through Wisdom
11. THEORY AND PRACTICAL OF EVERY ACTION
12. LOGICAL UNDERSTANDING OF THE SUPREME
13. THE IMPERISHABLE SUPREME
14. Yatra Nishadraj se Hanuman Ghat Tak
15. Yatra Karnatak Ghat se Raja Ghat Tak
16. Yatra Pandey Ghat se Prayagraj Ghat Tak
17. Yatra Ranjendra Prasad Ghat se Dattatreya Ghat Tak
18. YaatraSindhiya Ghat se Gwaliar Ghat Tak
19. Yatra Mangala Gauri Ghat se Hanuman Gadhi Ghat Tak
20. Yatra Gaay Ghat Se Nishad Ghat Tak
21. MAA GANGA, GHATEN EVM UTSAV
22. Ganga Arti Dev Deepavali evam Any Utsav
23. Potentials of Digitalized India
24. VEDIC CONSCIOUSNESS
25. A Brief Introduction to Vedic Science
26. Kashi ke Barah Jyotirling
27. IMPACT OF MOTIVATION
28. Let's have a Milky Way Journey
29. Color Therapy in a Nutshell

59.   "The Holistic Cow: A Look at the Physical, Spiritual, and Cultural Importance of Cows in India"

Contact

DR. JAGADEESH PILLAI

PhD in Vedic Science

Four Times Guinness World Record Holder

Winner of Mahatma Gandhi Vishwa Shanti Puraskar and Global Peace Ambassador

Gemology, Astro & Vastu Consultant - Spiritual Counselor

Consultant for designing World Record Ideas

Efficient Tarot Card Reader

9839093003

myrichindia@gmail.com

drjagadeeshpillai@facebook

drjagadeeshpillai@instagram

jagadeeshpillai@youtube

www. JAGADEESHPILLAI.com

|| LOKAHA SAMSTHAHA SUKHINO BHAVANTU ||

• 51 •

www.ingramcontent.com/pod-product-compliance
Lightning Source LLC
Chambersburg PA
CBHW031507150726

47990CB00007B/2910